a gift for

from

OTHER GIFTBOOKS BY HELEN EXLEY:
Young at heart
Men! by women
Over 30s' Jokes
A Spread of Over 40s' Jokes
A Triumph of Over 50s' Jokes
Old is Great!
Ms Murphy's Law
Happy Birthday, you poor old wreck

Published simultaneously in 2001 by Exley Publications Ltd in Great Britain, and Exley Publications LLC in the USA.

12   11   10   9   8   7

Design, selection and arrangement copyright © 2001 Helen Exley
Cartoons copyright © 1998 Rowan Barnes-Murphy
The moral right of the authors has been asserted.

ISBN 1-86187-165-1

Printed in China.

Exley Publications Ltd, 16 Chalk Hill, Watford, Herts WD19 4BG, UK.
Exley Publications LLC, 185 Main Street, Spencer, MA 01562, USA.
www.helenexleygiftbooks.com

Acknowledgements: The publishers are grateful for permission to reproduce copyright material. Whilst every effort has been made to trace copyright holders, we would be pleased to hear from any not here acknowledged. PAM BROWN, CHARLOTTE GRAY, STUART AND LINDA MACFARLANE, BILL STOTT: Used by permission.

Too Soon for a Mid-Life Crisis

Rowan Barnes-Murphy

≣ EXLEY

You're aging when your actions
creak louder than your words.

MILTON BERLE

When you are old
your body creaks and your
knees knock and your teeth
fall out.

ADRIAN TYDD, AGE 10,
FROM "HAPPY BIRTHDAY, YOU POOR OLD WRECK"

"You Know you're getting old
when everything hurts
and what doesn't hurt
doesn't work"

BOB HOPE

"MIDDL

UNUSUAL
MEDICAL
CONDITIONS

iS Mo.

AGE IS WHEN ANYTHING NEW YOU FEEL IS LIKELY TO BE A SYMPTOM."

LAURENCE J. PETER

"THERE ARE THREE SIGNS
of OLD AGE
LOSS of MEMORY
I forget THE OTHER TWO"

RED SKELTON

I used to be indecisive...
but now I'm not so sure....

BOSCOE PERTWEE

At my age I don't care
if my mind starts to wander
just as long
as it comes back again.

MIKE KNOWLES

You KNOW YOU'RE GETTING OLD
WHEN THE CANDLES
COST MORE THAN THE CAKE

Bob Hope

When you have a birthday
and you are middle-aged
your friends all clink their glasses
and cheer and it gives you a headache.

PHILLIP BROOKE, AGE 8,
FROM "HAPPY BIRTHDAY, YOU POOR OLD WRECK"

Just think, if only you could
snap your fingers on the birthday you
wanted and never grow any older! HUH!
Birthdays won't even let you do that
because you've got that much artheritis
your fingers won't snap.

SUSAN CURZON, AGE 12,
FROM "HAPPY BIRTHDAY, YOU POOR OLD WRECK"

"I HAVE EVERYTHING
I HAD 20 YEARS AGO
...ONLY IT'S ALL a BIT LOWER."

LOIS L. KAUF

Middle age is when
your age starts showing
around your middle.

BOB HOPE

Middle age is when
your wife tells you to
pull in your stomach,
and you already have.

JACK BARRY

"If I had my life to live again I'd make the same mistakes... only sooner."

TALLULAH BANKHEAD

Only the young die good.

OLIVER HERFORD

All the things
I really like to do
are either immoral,
illegal or fattening.

ALEXANDER WOOLLCOTT

If you're old enough
to know better,
you're too old to do it.

GEORGE BURNS

I'm at an age when my back goes out
more than I do.

PHYLLIS DILLER

Middle age is when you're willing
to get up and give your seat to
a lady and can't.

SAMMY KAY

You know you've reached middle age
when your weightlifting consists
merely of standing up.

BOB HOPE

I smoke cigars because at my age
if I don't have something to hang on to,
I might fall down.

GEORGE BURNS

"There are hills where none used to be"

PAM BROWN b 1928

Just about the time
when you realise you're
over-the-hill your brakes
give in.

AUTHOR UNKNOWN

Middle age is... when you are
warned to slow down
by a doctor instead of
a police officer.

SIDNEY BRODY

Middle age is...
when you need
to have a rest
after tying
your shoelaces.

MIKE KNOWLES

You know you're middle-aged
when the dog lets you
get to the stick first.

BILL STOTT

"It's so long since I've had sex I've forgotten who gets tied up."

JOAN RIVERS

You're past it...
when the spirit's willing but the
flesh is too flipping tired.

CHARLOTTE GRAY

You're middle aged...
when making love
turns you into a wild animal
– a sloth.

PAM BROWN, B.1928

At fifty you still get the urge – but can't
remember what for....

AUTHOR UNKNOWN

Old age? That's the period of life when
you buy a see-through nightgown
and then remember you don't know
anybody who can still see through one.

BETTE DAVIS

If the young
only knew;
if the old
only could.

FRENCH PROVERB

The important thing in acting
is to be able to laugh and cry.
If I have to cry, I think of my sex life.
If I have to laugh,
I think of my sex life.

GLENDA JACKSON

Don't worry about
avoiding temptation.
As you grow older,
it will avoid you.

JOEY ADAMS

After thirty, a body has a mind
of its own.

BETTE MIDLER

I'm the same weight as when I was
twenty-five. Unfortunately, at least
30% of it's in one place....

BILL STOTT,
FROM OVER 50s' JOKES

The older you get, the harder it is
to lose weight, because your body
has made friends with your fat.

LYNN ALPERN AND ESTHER BLUMENFELD

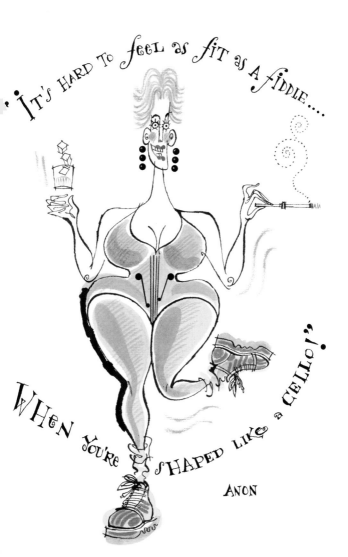

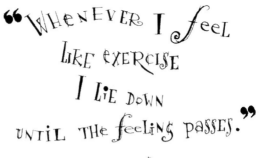

"Whenever I feel like exercise I lie down until the feeling passes."

ROBERT M HUTCHINS

The only reason I would take up jogging is so I could hear heavy breathing again.

ERMA BOMBECK

Middle age is when the best exercise is discretion.

LAURENCE J. PETER

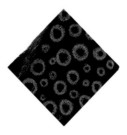

It's time to give up booze, sex,
over-eating, partying,
late nights etc.,
... on your next birthday.

STUART AND LINDA MACFARLANE

The only way to keep your health
is to eat what you don't want,
drink what you don't like,
and do what you'd rather not.

MARK TWAIN

"WHY EXERCISE?...

...If you're healthy ~ you don't need it...
...If you're sick ~ you shouldn't take it"

HENRY FORD

Early to rise and early to bed
Makes a man healthy and wealthy
and dead.

JAMES THURBER

Now I'm over fifty my doctor says I
should go out and get more fresh air
and exercise. I said, "All right, I'll drive
with the car window open."

ANGUS WALKER

"You're over the hill when
you feel like the morning after
and you can swear
you haven't been anywhere."

Laurence J. Peter

I don't feel old. In fact, I don't feel
anything till noon. Then it's time
for my nap.

BOB HOPE

Youth looks ahead,
old age looks back,
and middle age looks tired.

DEBBIE HANSEN

"OLD AGE
IS WHEN CANDLELIT TABLES
ARE NO LONGER ROMANTIC
BECAUSE YOU CAN'T
READ THE MENU"

LOIS L. KAUFMAN

Middle age is the time a guy starts
turning out lights for economic
rather than romantic reasons.

JOHN MARINO

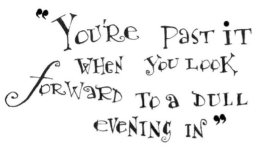

"You're past it when you look forward to a dull evening in"

PAM BROWN b.1928

Now that I can afford a big house, I don't have the energy to clean it.

DENISE TIFFANY

You know you are growing old when, confronted by a most beautiful dress, you read the label and decide you'd rather get the guttering mended.

PAM BROWN, B.1928

"I'M NOT aging I'M Marinating"

T-SHIRT SLOGAN

You know you're getting older when a fortune-teller offers to read your face.

J.K.N

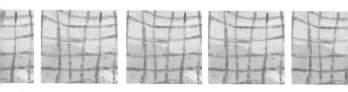

Middle age is... when you get white hairs
from worrying about your wrinkles.

PAM BROWN, B.1928

Middle age is when your old classmates
are so grey and wrinkled and bald
they don't recognize you.

BENNET CERF

The best thing that can happen to a
couple married for fifty years or more is
that they both grow near-sighted together.

LINDA FITERMAN

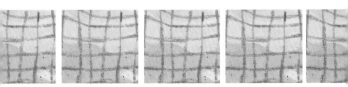

" You're Never Too Old
To Become Younger "

MAE WEST

Middle age is
when your hair
starts turning
from gray
to black.

AUTHOR UNKNOWN

Middle age is when instead of combing
your hair, you start "arranging" it.

HERBERT I. KAVET

Your doctor, your dentist, your plastic
surgeon, your beautician all
drink champagne on your birthday.

MARION C. GARRETTY

When I was twenty, getting ready
to go out took no time. Now
I'm forty, it takes two hours.
By the time I'm eighty, it won't be
worth going out!

BILL STOTT

THE SECRET of STAYING YOUNG...

...is to Live Honestly, eat slowly, sleep Sufficien

work industriously, worship faithfully...

...AND THEN...LIE ABOUT YOUR AGE

LUCILLE BALL

Allow me to put
the record straight.
I am forty-six and have been
for some years past.

ERICA JONG

When women pass thirty,
they first forget their age;
when forty, they forget
that they ever remembered it.

NINON DE LENCLOS

A diplomat is a man
who always remembers
a woman's birthday
but never
remembers her age.

ROBERT FROST

"Being an old Maid
is like death by drowning
a really delightful Sensation
after you have ceased
Struggling"

EDNA FERBER

Childhood: the time of life
when you make funny faces
in the mirror.
Middle age: the time of life
when the mirror gets even.

MICKEY MANSFIELD

There are three periods
in life: youth, middle age
and "how well you look."

NELSON A. ROCKEFELLER

At twenty we don't care
what the world thinks of us;
at thirty we start to worry about
what it thinks of us;
at forty we realize that it isn't thinking
of us at all.

L.C.

I don't know how you feel about old age,
but in my case I didn't even see it coming.
It hit me from the rear.

PHYLLIS DILLER

"THE BEST TUNES ARE PLAYED ON THE OLDEST fiddles."

SIGMUND ENGEL

Boys will be boys,
and so will a lot of
middle-aged men.

ELBERT HUBBARD

We all have flaws
and mine
is being wicked.

JAMES THURBER

Sex with older men?
I say grab it. But if your man
has had a heart attack
don't... try to jump start his
pacemaker... whisper... "This could
be your last one, let's make it good."

PHYLLIS DILLER

The only people who really
adore being young
are the middle-aged.

PAM BROWN, B.1928

Age is strictly a case
of mind over matter.
If you don't mind,
it doesn't matter.

JACK BENNY

One of the many things
nobody ever tells you about
middle age is that it's such a nice
change from being young.

DOROTHY CANFIELD FISHER

"IT TAKES A LONG TIME
TO GROW OLD"

PABLO PICASSO

"Time and Trouble will
Tame an advanced
young woman, but
an advanced old woman
is uncontrollable by
any earthly force"

DOROTHY L. SAYERS

If you want a thing well done,
get a couple of old broads
to do it.

BETTE DAVIS

Old age is no place for sissies.

BETTE DAVIS

Age is not important
unless you're a cheese.

HELEN HAYES

When somebody says to me, which they
do like every five years, "How does it feel
to be over the hill?" my response is, "I'm
just heading up the mountain."

JOAN BAEZ

If you think your mid-life crisis is bad just wait to see how dreadful your old-life crisis will be.

STUART AND LINDA MACFARLANE

Cheer up! The worst is still to come!

PHILANDEER CHASE JOHNSON

The really frightening thing about middle age is the knowledge that you'll grow out of it.

DORIS DAY

This is a youth-orientated society, and the joke is on them because youth is a disease from which we all recover.

DOROTHY FULDHEIM

Anyone can get old.
All you have to do is live long enough.

GROUCHO MARX

"You're at that age when everything
Mother Nature gave you Father Time
is taking away"

MILTON BERLE

The denunciation of the young
is a necessary part of the hygiene
of older people, and greatly assists the
circulation of the blood.

LOGAN PEARSALL SMITH

Middle age is when you stop criticizing
the old generation and start criticizing
the younger one.

L.C.

They tell you that you'll lose your
mind when you grow older.
What they don't tell you is that you
won't miss it very much.

MALCOLM COWLEY

I am not young enough
to know everything.

SIR JAMES M. BARRIE

When I was young,
I was told:
"You'll see when you're fifty."
I am fifty and I haven't
seen a thing.

ERIK SATIE

If we could sell our experiences for
what they cost us we'd be millionaires.

ABIGAIL VAN BUREN

EXPERIENCE
IS THE NAME
RYONE GIVES
O THEIR
ISTAKES "

OSCAR WILDE

... the young fool
has first to grow up
to be an old fool to
realise what a damn fool
he was when he was a
young fool.

HAROLD MACMILLAN

There is no fool like an old fool –
you can't beat experience.

JACOB M. BRAUDE

No one is ever old enough to know better.

HOLBROOK JACKSON

"Aren't I Wise?"

Old is... when you look
in the mirror and think
to yourself "Aren't I wise".

MARCELLA MARKHAM,
FROM "OLD IS GREAT"

Middle age is when
you know all the answers
and nobody asks you
the questions.

BOB PHILLIPS

Middle age is... when
you start to say
things like "in my day."

PAM BROWN, B.1928

They say that life begins
at forty but so do lumbago,
bad eyesight, arthritis,
and the habit of telling
the same story three times
to the same person.

L.C.

"I'm still chasing pretty girls
I don't remember what for
but I'm still chasing them."

JOE E LEWIS

By the time a man is wise enough
to watch his step, he's too old
to go anywhere.

JOEY ADAMS

At my age, when a girl flirts with me in
the movies, she's after my popcorn.

MILTON BERLE

First you forget names,
then you forget faces, then you forget to
pull your zipper up, then
you forget to pull your zipper down.

LEO ROSENBERG

It's hard to be nostalgic when you can't remember anything.

AUTHOR UNKNOWN

You know you're getting older
when you try to straighten out
the wrinkles in your socks
and discover
you're not wearing any.

LEONARD L. KNOTT

What's the good
of having something
to look forward to,
if I can't remember
what it was?

ASHLEIGH BRILLIANT

"ETERNITY'S A TERRIB[LE]

... never think of the future.
It comes soon enough.

ALBERT EINSTEIN

One of the saddest things
of growing old is that
you might have an illness
that cannot be cured
and the doctor might say,
"We are very sorry, very, very,
but we are going to have to
put you down."

ALEX STANGER, AGE 7,
FROM "HAPPY BIRTHDAY, YOU POOR
OLD WRECK."

I ME[

HOUGHT

"WHERE IS IT ALL GOING TO END?"

TOM STOPPARD

Old age isn't so bad
when you consider
the alternative.

MAURICE CHEVALIER

Better a bald head
than no head at all.

MAURICE CHEVALIER

Quit worrying
about your health.
It'll go away.

ROBERT ORBEN

Death is nature's way of telling you
to slow down.

GRAFFITI

I get up every morning and dust off my wits,
go pick up the paper and read the "o-bits."
If my name isn't there I know I'm not dead;
I get a good breakfast and go back to bed.

AUTHOR UNKNOWN

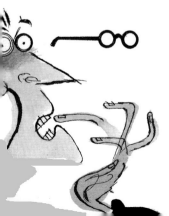

There is no cure for birth and death, save to enjoy the interval.

GEORGE SANTAYANA

"YOUNG ...... OLD

"JUST.... WORDS...."

GEORGE BURNS

My problem
is reconciling my
gross habits with
my net income.

ERROL FLYNN

Last Will and Testament:
Being of sound mind,
I spent all my money.

AUTHOR UNKNOWN

HELEN EXLEY

Helen Exley has been collecting
and editing material for her
books for twenty-five years and
still enjoys complete involvement
with each new title.

Her individually conceived and
selected books have now sold
forty-one million copies since
Exley Publications was formed in
1976. They are now found on
bookstalls as far apart as Beijing
and Istanbul, Helsinki
and Rio de Janeiro.

ROWAN BARNES-MURPHY

Rowan Barnes-Murphy's cartoons are wicked, spiky and frayed at the edges.

His fantastically well-observed
characters are hugely popular
and have been used to advertise a
diverse range of products such
as cars, clothes and phones,
supermarkets, bank accounts
and greeting cards.
For more information on the range
of greetings cards and related
products contact
Lincoln Exley Designs Ltd,
Suite 4, Kings Court,
153 High Street, Watford,
Herts WD17 23ZY, UK
Tel: (0) 1923 246005